KENDRICK
GEORGE

Murcia, Spain Travel Guide

Discover the Charm of Spain's Southeast.

COPYRIGHT

Table of Contents

INTRODUCTION

Welcome to Murcia!

Welcome to the Murcia Travel Guide: Discover the Charm of Spain's Southeast. Murcia, located in southern Spain, is a hidden treasure that is frequently overshadowed by its more well-known neighbors. However, for those willing to explore, it provides an intriguing combination of rich history, lively culture, and breathtaking natural beauty. Whether you're an experienced traveler or beginning on your first excursion, this book will be your trusty friend as you discover Murcia's numerous marvels.

Introduction to Murcia.

Murcia, the seat of the autonomous community of the same name, is a city that perfectly blends the ancient and contemporary.

Murcia is rich in history, dating back to 825 AD when the Moors founded the city. Its architecture displays a diverse range of influences, from the opulence of its Baroque church to the tranquil beauty of its Moorish homes. Murcia, however, is more than simply a historical city; it is a dynamic, contemporary metropolis renowned for its colorful festivals, busy markets, and a booming culinary scene that celebrates the abundance of its lush fields.

Beyond the city, Murcia has a diversified environment. From the gorgeous beaches of the Costa Cálida to the craggy mountains and verdant valleys in the interior, there is something for every type of traveler. The mild Mediterranean environment offers nice weather throughout the year, making it a perfect location for both leisure and adventure.

Why should you visit Murcia?

Why should you visit Murcia? Simply told, Murcia provides a real Spanish experience, which is becoming more uncommon in today's world. You may wonder through historic neighborhoods without being bothered by the masses of visitors who frequent more famous places. You may enjoy traditional cuisine cooked with locally sourced ingredients, sample some of Spain's best wines, and immerse yourself in the colorful local culture. Murcia's festivals, such as the Spring Festival (Fiestas de Primavera) and

Holy Week (Semana Santa) processions, are magnificent festivities that provide a profound understanding of the region's traditions and communal spirit.

Murcia is a nature lover's heaven. The area is home to various natural parks, which provide excellent chances for hiking, bird viewing, and admiring stunning scenery. Water sports enthusiasts will enjoy the Mar Menor, Europe's biggest saltwater lagoon, which is ideal for sailing, kayaking, and windsurfing. Golfers, too, are spoiled for choice with so many world-class golf courses.

How to Use This Guide?

This book is intended to be your thorough companion as you discover the various elements of Murcia. We've categorized the information so that you can easily discover what you're looking for, whether you're planning a vacation or are currently in Murcia and searching for things to do.

- **Getting There and Around Murcia:** Start here to learn about the best ways to travel to and within Murcia, including tips on public transportation and car rentals.
- **Essential Information:** Equip yourself with practical information about currency, language, health, and safety.

- **Where to Stay:** Find recommendations for accommodations to suit every budget, from luxury hotels to charming guesthouses.
- **Top Attractions:** Discover the must-see sights, from historical landmarks to cultural hotspots.
- **Cultural Experiences:** Delve into the heart of Murcia's vibrant culture, with insights into local festivals, art, and traditions.
- **Outdoor Activities:** Explore the natural beauty of the region with our guide to outdoor adventures.
- **Day Trips and Excursions:** Plan your excursions to nearby gems, ensuring you make the most of your visit.
- **Food and Drink:** Savor Murcia's culinary delights with our recommendations on where to eat and drink.
- **Shopping**: Learn where to find the best local crafts, markets, and shopping districts.
- **Nightlife and Entertainment:** Discover the best spots for an exciting night out.
- **Family-Friendly Activities:** Find activities that the whole family can enjoy.
- **Seasonal Guide:** Get tips on the best times to visit and what to pack for each season.
- **Practical Tips:** Handy advice for a smooth and enjoyable trip.

- **Itineraries:** Suggested itineraries to help you plan your visit based on your interests and the time you have available.

Chapter 1: Getting to and Around Murcia Airports and Flights.

Murcia is serviced by Región de Murcia International Airport (RMU), commonly known as Murcia-Corvera Airport. This new airport, located about 25 kilometers south of Murcia, opened in 2019 and has rapidly established itself as a major gateway for both local and international visitors. Major airlines fly regularly between Murcia and a variety of European countries, including the United Kingdom, Germany, and the Netherlands. During the peak tourist season, more charter flights are available, making it even simpler to visit this attractive location.

Upon arrival, you will discover a variety of conveniences to guarantee a smooth start to your journey. The airport has car rental services, taxis, and shuttle buses that may transport you straight to Murcia's city center or other surrounding attractions. For those wishing to save travel expenses, numerous budget airlines fly to Murcia, offering it an economical entry point into southern Spain.

Train and Bus Services.

Murcia has an efficient and dependable rail and bus network, making it convenient to travel both within the province and across Spain. The major rail station, Murcia del Carmen, is situated immediately south of the city center. It is operated by Renfe, Spain's national railway corporation, and provides frequent service to major cities such Madrid, Barcelona, and Valencia. The high-speed AVE trains provide a swift and pleasant ride, greatly decreasing travel time to several important cities.

Murcia's bus network is substantial, with various firms operating regional, national, and international routes. ALSA, one of Spain's leading bus carriers, offers regular service to cities across Spain and even to neighboring countries. The primary bus station, Estación de Autobuses de Murcia, is ideally placed in the city center, making it simple to take a bus to your destination.

The city's bus system, run by Latbus, is a great method to get about Murcia. The buses are contemporary and air-conditioned, and they serve all main regions of the city, including important tourist destinations and residential communities.

Car Rental and Driving Tips.

Renting a vehicle is a popular choice for those who want to explore Murcia and its surroundings at their own leisure. Several automobile rental businesses operate at Murcia-Corvera Airport and in the city center. Booking in advance is encouraged, particularly during high tourist season, to assure availability and the best pricing.

Driving in Murcia is quite simple, with well-kept roads and adequate signs. However, there are a few suggestions to bear in mind:

- **Speed Limits:** In cities, the speed limit is usually 50 km/h, but on highways it varies from 90 to 120 km/h.
- **Parking:** Parking in the city center may be difficult, particularly during peak times. Look for public parking facilities or allocated parking spaces. Blue lines on the road denote paid parking areas.
- **Tolls:** Some Spanish roadways are toll roads. Be prepared to pay tolls in cash or with a credit card, and consider using a GPS to help you navigate.

Exploring the area by automobile allows you to see off-the-beaten-path destinations like the gorgeous Ricote Valley or the stunning Costa Cálida beaches.

Public Transportation in Murcia.

Murcia's public transportation system is well-developed, with several alternatives for moving about the city and its surroundings. LATBUS operates city buses that span broad routes and offer a simple method to commute between various regions of Murcia. Tickets may be paid on the bus, and there are discounts available for repeated rides.

Murcia has both buses and a tram system called Tranvía de Murcia. The tram route links significant places, such as the university, commercial malls, and residential neighborhoods. It's a clean, efficient, and environmentally responsible way to get about the city.

Taxis are easily accessible throughout Murcia and may be hailed on the street, ordered over the phone, or via mobile applications. They are a practical choice for short excursions or for transporting bags. Taxi prices are controlled, with meters used to compute the fee depending on distance and time.

Walking and Biking.

Murcia is a pedestrian-friendly city with a small and easily navigated city core. Many of the prominent attractions, like the Murcia Cathedral and the Real Casino de Murcia, are within walking distance of one another. Strolling around the city's lovely streets enables you to properly appreciate its ancient architecture and dynamic street scene.

For those who prefer riding, Murcia has an expanding network of bike lanes and pathways. The city's flat landscape is great for riding, and various bike rental businesses provide reasonable pricing. In addition, MuyBici, the public bike-sharing system, provides a convenient and environmentally beneficial way to explore the city. Bikes may be leased at many stations and returned at any other station, making them an adaptable alternative for short journeys or a day of touring.

Traveling to and around Murcia is simple and easy, whether you like to fly, take the train or bus, drive, or use public transit. With so many possibilities, you can simply modify your trip plans to meet your needs and experience all this gorgeous area has to offer.

Chapter 2: Essential Murcia Information.

Currency and Money Matters.

To guarantee a smooth and comfortable vacation to Murcia, get acquainted with the local currency and banking norms.

Currency.

The euro (€) is Spain's official currency. Banknotes are available in denominations of 5, 10, 20, 50, 100, 200, and 500 euros, and coins are available in 1, 2, 5, 10, 20, and 50 cents, as well as 1 and 2 euros.

Changing Money.

Banks, currency exchange offices, and big hotels all provide money exchange services. Banks normally provide the best exchange rates, but may charge a service fee. Currency exchange offices, or "cambios," are often available in tourist locations and provide a quick option, albeit their rates may be somewhat more. It's a good idea to convert a little amount of money before your travel to cover early expenditures like airport transfers.

ATMs.

ATMs are extensively distributed across Murcia, notably at the airport, city center, and important tourist sites. Most ATMs accept foreign credit and debit cards, including Visa, MasterCard, and Maestro. Check with your home bank before your trip to see whether they impose any international transaction or ATM use fees. It's a good idea to advise your bank about your trip intentions to prevent problems with card use overseas.

Credit and Debit Cards.

Credit and debit cards are frequently accepted across Murcia, notably at hotels, restaurants, and bigger retailers. Smaller restaurants, markets, and rural locations may prefer cash, so bring some euros with you. Always bring a form of identification, such as a passport or driver's license, since certain establishments may need it for card purchases.

Tipping.

Tipping in Spain is not as common as in other nations, yet it is valued for excellent service. In restaurants, giving a tip of 5-10% of the bill is customary, particularly if the service was excellent. In cafés and bars, rounding up the tab or leaving a modest change is enough. Rounding up to the closest euro is common practice among taxi drivers.

VAT refunds.

Non-EU travelers are entitled to a VAT refund on purchases above a particular threshold (currently €90.15). To be eligible, you must shop at shops that participate in the VAT refund program and get a Tax-Free Shopping form. To claim your refund, present the completed form, along with your purchases and receipts, to the airport's customs office when you exit the EU.

Language and Useful Phrases.

Spanish is Murcia's official language, and although English is widely spoken in tourist areas, learning a few basic Spanish phrases may dramatically improve your travel experience and help you interact with people.

- Basic Spanish Phrases.
- Here are some keywords to get you started:
- Hello: Hola
- Goodbye: Adiós
- Please: Por favor
- Thank you: Gracias
- You're welcome: De nada
- Yes: Sí
- No: No

- Excuse me: Perdón / Disculpe
- I'm sorry: Lo siento
- Do you speak English?: ¿Habla inglés?
- I don't understand: No entiendo.
- How much does it cost?: ¿Cuánto cuesta?
- Where is...?: ¿Dónde está...?
- I would like...: Me gustaría…

Pronunciation Tips

Spanish pronunciation is generally phonetic, meaning words are pronounced as they are written. Here are a few tips to help you with pronunciation:

- The letter "h" is silent (e.g., "hola" is pronounced "oh-la").
- The letter "j" is pronounced like the English "h" (e.g., "jugo" is pronounced "hoo-go").
- The letter "ll" is pronounced like the English "y" (e.g., "llama" is pronounced "ya-ma").
- The letter "ñ" is pronounced like the "ny" in "canyon" (e.g., "año" is pronounced "ahn-yo").

Cultural Etiquette in Murcia.

When speaking Spanish, it is essential to be courteous and respectful. Address strangers and elderly folks with formal titles like "Señor" (Mr.) and "Señora" (Mrs.). Spaniards generally greet one another with a handshake or, in more casual situations, a kiss on each cheek. Maintaining eye contact throughout a conversation demonstrates attentiveness and respect.

Learning More Spanish.

If you want to study more Spanish before or during your vacation, try language learning applications such as Duolingo, Babbel, or Rosetta Stone. Additionally, having a small phrasebook might be quite useful for rapid reference.

Language Resources in Murcia.

Murcia is home to a number of language schools and cultural institutes that teach Spanish to foreign students. Participating in a short course or language exchange program may be an enjoyable and intensive way to improve your Spanish and meet new people.

Understanding the local currency and learning a few basic Spanish phrases can help you have a relaxing and happy time in Murcia. Embracing the local language and customs not only enhances your trip experience, but also builds a stronger bond with the lively culture and kind people of this lovely region.

Health and Safety Healthcare Services.

Murcia provides outstanding healthcare facilities, with both public and private hospitals, clinics, and pharmacies widely available. The Spanish National Health System (SNS) provides public healthcare, including high-quality medical services. EU people possessing a European Health Insurance Card (EHIC) can use these services, however non-EU travelers should have full travel insurance that covers medical costs.

Pharmacies.

Pharmacies, known as "farmacias," are widely available across Murcia. They are often marked with a green cross and provide over-the-counter drugs and health advice. Most pharmacies have typical business hours, although there are always 24-hour choices accessible on a rotating basis, called "farmacia de guardia." A list of these is frequently put on the drugstore door.

Vaccination and Health Precautions.

No special vaccinations are necessary for travel to Murcia, although normal immunizations like MMR, tetanus, and flu injections should be kept up to date. The tap water in Murcia is safe to drink, however bottled water is readily available if preferred. Use sunscreen and remain hydrated, particularly during the hot summer months.

Safety Tips.

Murcia is considered a safe destination with a low crime rate. However, standard precautions should be taken to ensure your safety:

- **Personal Belongings:** Keep an eye on your personal belongings, especially in crowded areas such as markets, festivals, and public transportation.
- **Pickpocketing:** Be aware of pickpockets in tourist-heavy areas. Use a money belt or cross-body bag to keep your valuables secure.
- **Emergency Numbers:** The general emergency number in Spain is 112, which can be dialed for police, fire, or medical emergencies.

Local Customs and Etiquette

Understanding and respecting local customs and etiquette will improve your trip experience and allow you to connect with the people of Murcia.

Greetings.

Spaniards are cordial and friendly, frequently greeting one another with a handshake or a kiss on both cheeks (beginning with the right cheek). A handshake is ideal for first-time meetings or in a more official situation.

Dinner Etiquette.

Meals in Spain are communal occasions, and it is customary to share meals, particularly tapas. Here are some eating etiquette suggestions:

- **Table Manners:** Wait for the host to begin eating before you start. Keep your hands visible on the table, but not your elbows.

- **Tipping:** Tipping is optional but appreciated for good service. A 5-10% tip is usual at restaurants. In cafés and bars, rounding up the tab or leaving a modest change is enough.

- **Meal Times:** Spaniards eat later than most other countries. Lunch (la comida) is normally served between 1:30 PM and 3:30 PM, while supper (la cena) begins about 8:30 PM and can go as late as 11:00 PM.

Dress Code:

While Murcia is generally laid-back, wearing properly and appropriately is welcomed. Beachwear should be limited to the beach or pool area. When visiting holy locations, keep your shoulders and knees covered as a gesture of respect.

Social norms.

- **Personal Space:** Spaniards are quite touchy and may approach more closely than other cultures are used to.
- **Punctuality:** While social activities might have flexible times, being on time for business meetings and official engagements is essential.
- **Noise Levels:** Spaniards are expressive and vivacious, and you'll often hear spirited discussions and laughing in public places.

Emergency Contacts.

In case of emergencies, it's crucial to know the local contact numbers and locations where you can get help quickly.

Emergency Numbers

- General Emergency: 112 (Police, Fire, Medical)
- Police: 091 (National Police), 092 (Local Police)
- Fire Department: 080
- Medical Emergency: 061

Hospitals and Medical Centers.

Here are a few major hospitals and medical centers in Murcia:

- Hospital General Universitario Reina Sofía: Address: Avenida Intendente Jorge Palacios, 30003 Murcia. Phone: +34 968 358 500

- Hospital Morales Meseguer: Address: Calle Marqués de los Vélez, s/n, 30008 Murcia. Phone: +34 968 360 000

- Hospital Mesa del Castillo: Address: Calle de la Mar, 8, 30003 Murcia. Phone: +34 968 222 214

Pharmacies.

For 24-hour pharmacies, look for the "farmacia de guardia" sign or check online for the nearest one on duty.

Embassies and Consulates.

If you lose your passport or need assistance from your home country, here are the contact details for a few major embassies:

- **United Kingdom:** British Consulate Alicante, Address: Plaza de Calvo Sotelo, 1, 03001 Alicante. Phone: +34 965 21 60 22.

- **United States:** U.S. Consulate General Barcelona, Address: Paseo Reina Elisenda de Montcada, 23, 08034 Barcelona. Phone: +34 933 42 64 00.

- **Canada:** Canadian Consulate Barcelona, Address: Calle de Nápoles, 188, 08013 Barcelona. Phone: +34 932 02 24 04.

Being well-prepared with important health and safety information, understanding local traditions, and having emergency contacts on hand helps guarantee a safe, respectful, and pleasurable stay in Murcia. Accept the local culture, be educated, and enjoy your time touring this stunning area.

Chapter 3: Where To Stay in Murcia Spain.

Murcia has a wide variety of lodgings to meet any traveler's demands and budget. From opulent hotels to lovely mid-range alternatives to economical budget lodgings, you'll discover the ideal spot to stay while visiting this stunning area.

Luxury Hotels.

Murcia's finest hotels provide great service, attractive accommodations, and first-rate facilities. Here are a few of the top choices:

1. Hotel Nelva.

Hotel Nelva is located in the city center and blends contemporary style with comfort and convenience. Guests may enjoy large rooms with modern décor, a lovely outdoor pool, and a well-equipped fitness center. The on-site restaurant provides a gourmet dining experience, with a menu that includes Mediterranean and local specialties.

2. Occidental Murcia, Siete Coronas.

Occidental Murcia Siete Coronas, located on the banks of the Segura River, is a landmark hotel renowned for its refined environment and exceptional service. The stylishly designed suites have breathtaking views of the river or city, and the hotel's amenities include a gourmet restaurant, a sophisticated bar, and substantial meeting facilities. Its central position provides it an excellent base for seeing Murcia's attractions.

3. Parador de Lorca.

Consider staying at the Parador de Lorca if you want an unforgettable experience. This premium hotel is set on the grounds of Lorca Castle, providing stunning vistas and a strong feeling of history. The rooms combine contemporary amenities with historical elegance, and the hotel has a spa, an outdoor pool, and a restaurant that serves regional cuisine. It is an excellent alternative for individuals who want to immerse themselves in the region's rich cultural history.

Mid-range Hotels.

Murcia's mid-range hotels provide great value, with comfortable lodgings and a variety of services without breaking the budget. Here are a few common options:

1. Hotel Casa Emilio.

This lovely hotel is situated between the Segura River and the Floridablanca Garden, offering a tranquil environment while being accessible to the city center. Hotel Casa Emilio has clean, comfortable rooms with classic design, a nice on-site café, and friendly, attentive service. It's a fantastic alternative for tourists seeking a comfortable environment at a fair price.

2. Catalonia Conde de Floridablanca.

Catalonia Conde de Floridablanca, located within a short walk from the historic city center, has contemporary accommodations and a warm environment. The hotel has a rooftop patio, a small gym, and an on-site restaurant that serves a delectable breakfast buffet and Mediterranean cuisine. Its handy location and nice facilities make it a popular destination for both visitors and business travelers.

3. El Churra Hotel.

El Churra is a well-known hotel that provides friendly welcome and pleasant rooms. The large rooms are nicely designed and provide contemporary facilities. The hotel also has a famous restaurant that specializes in Murcian cuisine, offering visitors a genuine dining experience. Its closeness to the city center and key attractions makes it a good base for exploring Murcia.

Budget Accommodations.

Travelers on a budget will discover a variety of economical lodgings in Murcia, ranging from hostels to budget hotels that provide excellent value without sacrificing comfort.

1. Ibis Murcia.

Ibis Murcia, located just outside of the city center, is a solid alternative for budget-conscious guests. The hotel has clean, contemporary rooms with basic facilities including free Wi-Fi and a flat-screen TV. Guests may enjoy a continental breakfast buffet and a 24-hour snack bar. Its low prices and handy location make it a popular choice for both short and long-term visits.

2. The Cathedral Hostel

The Cathedral Hostel offers a more sociable environment. This hostel, located in the center of Murcia, provides both dormitory-style and private rooms at extremely moderate prices. The welcoming ambiance and public amenities, such as a shared kitchen and lounge, make it simple to meet other tourists. The hostel also arranges activities and trips, giving visitors the opportunity to discover Murcia and meet new people.

3. Pension Segura.

Pension Segura is a family-run guesthouse situated near the Segura River that provides modest yet decent lodgings. The rooms are simple but tidy, with private bathrooms and complimentary Wi-Fi. The pension features an on-site café where visitors may have breakfast and light meals. Its central location and reasonable costs make it an excellent choice for budget tourists wishing to stay near Murcia's major attractions.

Hostels and Guesthouses in Murcia.

Murcia's hostels and guesthouses provide economical and pleasant lodging for budget-conscious visitors and those looking for a sociable environment. Here are a few of the top choices:

1. *Cathedral Hostel.*

The Cathedral Hostel, located in the center of Murcia, is a popular destination for backpackers and lone travelers. The hostel provides both dormitory-style and private rooms at moderate prices. The welcoming ambiance and public amenities, such as a shared kitchen and lounge, make it simple to meet other tourists. The hostel also arranges activities and trips, giving visitors the opportunity to discover Murcia and meet new people. Its central position ensures that significant attractions such as the Murcia Cathedral and the Real Casino de Murcia are just a short walk away.

2. *La Casa verde*

La Casa Verde is an unusual eco-hostel situated just outside the city center. Surrounded by beautiful gardens, this lovely hostel provides a tranquil getaway with an emphasis on sustainability. Guests may select between dormitory beds and individual rooms, all designed in a bohemian style. The hostel has a shared kitchen, a bar, and a variety of outdoor leisure spots, including hammocks and a patio. La Casa Verde is a colorful and pleasant location to stay, with regular activities including yoga sessions and live music.

3. Pension Segura.

Pension Segura is a family-run guesthouse situated near the Segura River that provides modest yet decent lodgings. The rooms are simple but tidy, with private bathrooms and complimentary Wi-Fi. The pension features an on-site café where visitors may have breakfast and light meals. Its central location and reasonable costs make it an excellent choice for budget tourists wishing to stay near Murcia's major attractions. This guesthouse's warm and friendly environment provides a comfortable and homelike stay.

Unique Stays: Boutique Hotels and Villas.

Murcia's boutique hotels and villas provide a more distinctive and customized experience, with charm, elegance, and unique character. Here are some noteworthy choices:

1. Hotel Arco de San Juan.

Hotel Arco de San Juan, housed in a magnificently renovated 17th-century edifice, blends ancient grandeur with contemporary comfort. Each room is distinctively furnished, combining traditional features with modern accents. The hotel has a sophisticated bar and a garden where guests may unwind and have a drink. Its prominent position, adjacent to Plaza Cardenal Belluga and the Murcia Cathedral, making it an excellent starting point for visiting the city's cultural attractions.

2. La Huerta El Molino.

Consider staying in a villa at La Huerta El Molino for a really unforgettable experience. This beautiful rural hideaway is housed in a refurbished ancient mill, surrounded by orchards and gardens. The homes are attractively designed, blending rustic charm and contemporary comforts. Guests may enjoy a private pool, a fully furnished kitchen, and outside eating options. La Huerta El Molino, located only a short drive from Murcia city, provides a calm vacation with convenient access to the region's attractions.

3. Casa Almendro.

Casa Almendro is a boutique hotel in the charming hamlet of Ricote, nestled inside the breathtaking Ricote Valley. This modest hotel has wonderfully designed rooms, each with a distinct flair and charm. The hotel has a beautiful garden, a sun deck, and a small pool. Guests may have a great breakfast produced from local ingredients before exploring the nearby area, which is ideal for hiking and outdoor sports. Casa Almendro offers an intimate and luxurious experience in a peaceful environment.

4. *Aire Murcia.*

Aire Murcia is a modern boutique hotel renowned for its chic decor and customized service. Each room is uniquely designed with contemporary furniture and creative elements. The hotel has a rooftop patio with panoramic views of the city, a stylish bar, and a gourmet restaurant offering unique cuisine. Aire Murcia, located in the center of Murcia, is ideal for tourists seeking a classy and one-of-a-kind experience while remaining accessible to the city's dynamic cultural scene.

Choosing the Right Accommodation in Murcia.

Choosing the correct location to stay is an important aspect of arranging your vacation to Murcia. The varied choice of hotels provided ensures that there is something for everyone's budget, preference, and travel style. Here's how to find the finest hotels for your preferences, as well as some booking tips and methods to make things simpler and less expensive.

Choosing the Right Accommodations.

Identify your priorities: Before arranging your stay, think about what is most essential to you in your accommodation. Are you seeking luxury, convenience, low-cost choices, or a unique experience? Here are some questions to help you make your decision:

- Do you like to stay in the city center, near main attractions, restaurants, and nightlife?
- Are you seeking for a peaceful escape away from the city, maybe in the countryside?
- Do you need certain facilities, such as a swimming pool, a fitness facility, or free WiFi?
- Are you traveling with family or a group and need bigger accommodations or unique facilities?

Consider the kind of accommodation.

Murcia has a variety of lodgings, each with its unique advantages:
- Luxury hotels are ideal for individuals who want high-end facilities, great service, and prominent locations.
- Mid-Range Hotels: Offer a pleasant stay with adequate facilities for a fair price.
- Budget Accommodations: Ideal for tourists trying to save money, including hostels and guesthouses.

- Boutique hotels and villas provide one-of-a-kind, individualized experiences complete with attractive décor and special amenities.

Research the location.

our accommodation's location might have a big influence on your trip experience. Staying near the city center gives you convenient access to major attractions, restaurants, and public transit. If you want a calmer setting, look for lodgings on the outskirts or in surrounding towns that provide peace and magnificent scenery.

Read the reviews and ratings.

Reading previous guests' reviews might give vital information about the accommodation's quality and service. Websites such as TripAdvisor, Booking.com, and Google Reviews provide thorough input from travelers, covering both advantages and negatives. Pay attention to recent reviews for the most up-to-date viewpoint.

Check for special requirements.

Make sure the hotel fits any specific needs you may have, such as accessibility features for disabled travelers, pet-friendly regulations if you're traveling with a pet, or family-friendly facilities if you're traveling with kids.

Booking Tips & Tricks

- **Book early.**

  To get the greatest pricing and availability, book your hotel as soon as possible, particularly during peak travel seasons or major events and festivals. Early reservations sometimes include savings or special deals.

- **Use Comparison Sites.**

  Websites like Booking.com, Expedia, and Hotels.com enable you to compare pricing, features, and locations among different lodging options. These services also include user reviews and ratings, allowing you to make an educated selection.

- **Search for deals and discounts.**

  Check for special offers, discount coupons, or package packages that include lodging, transportation, and activities. Signing up for travel website newsletters or hotel loyalty programs might also lead to unique bargains.

- **Consider flexible booking options.**

  Choose lodgings with flexible booking policies, which enable you to change or cancel your reservation without penalty. This flexibility is especially important if your vacation plans alter suddenly.

- *Verify Direct Booking Benefits.*

  Booking directly via the hotel's website may provide extra perks such as complimentary breakfast, room upgrades, or better cancellation policies. Always compare direct booking costs to those found on third-party websites.

- *Use Credit Card Rewards.*

  Many credit cards include travel rewards or cash back when booking hotels. Check to see if your credit card offers any travel bonuses or connections with certain hotels so you can take advantage of any discounts or perks.

- *Read the fine print.*

  Before confirming your reservation, carefully read the terms and conditions, including cancellation policies, extra costs (such as resort fees or taxes), and any house rules for your stay. Understanding this information might help you avoid unexpected expenditures or complications throughout your vacation.

- *Contact the accommodation.*

  If you have any unique requests or inquiries, please contact the accommodation directly. They may give information on hotel availability, special requests, and any current deals that may not be advertised online.

- ***Consider other accommodations.***
  If standard hotels are out of your price range, try vacation rentals (Airbnb, VRBO), hostels, or guesthouses. These solutions may provide one-of-a-kind experiences while also being less expensive.

Identifying your preferences, investigating multiple possibilities, and utilizing these booking tips and tactics can help you locate the ideal place to stay that increases your vacation experience while being within your budget. Enjoy your stay in this stunning and dynamic area!

Murcia's zoos and aquariums

Chapter 4: Murcia's Top Attractions.

Murcia is a treasure mine of historical and cultural sites that provide insight into its rich history. This chapter covers the best sights to see, along with practical information to help you organize your trip.

Murcia Cathedral.

Murcia Cathedral, also known as the Cathedral Church of Saint Mary in Murcia, is an architectural marvel that combines Gothic, Renaissance, and  Baroque styles. Its construction started in 1394 and took almost three centuries to finish, yielding an impressive collection of artistic components.

Highlights.

- Bell Tower: Standing 93 meters tall, it provides panoramic views of the city. It is the second-tallest cathedral tower in Spain.
- Chapel of the Vélez: Known for its beautiful Gothic design.
- Baroque Façade: A stunningly elaborate entryway that is a masterpiece of Baroque architecture.

Practical information.

- Address: Plaza del Cardenal Belluga, 30001 Murcia

- Monday through Saturday, 7:00 AM to 1:00 PM and 5:00 PM to 8:00 PM. Sundays and public holidays: 8:00 AM to 1:00 PM and 5:00 PM to 8:00 PM.
- Admission is free, but contributions are requested.
- Tips: Go early in the morning to avoid crowds and have a tranquil experience. Guided tours are offered and highly recommended for understanding the history and architecture.

Real Casino of Murcia.

The Real Casino de Murcia, founded in 1847, is a social club rather than a gaming establishment. It's one of Murcia's most iconic structures, blending modernist and eclectic architectural elements.

Highlights

- The Arab Courtyard is inspired by the Alhambra in Granada and has exquisite Islamic-style décor.
- The library is a luxurious area with an extensive collection of old books and stunning oak bookcases.

- A ballroom is a lavish area used for numerous social gatherings that is decorated with exquisite chandeliers and mirrors.

Practical information.

- Location: Calle Trapería 18, 30001 Murcia.
- Open Monday through Sunday from 10:30 a.m. to 7:00 p.m.
- Admission costs about €5 per person and includes an audio tour.
- Tips: Allow at least an hour to tour the inside. Photography is permitted, so bring your camera to catch the fine details.

Salzillo Museum.

The Salzillo Museum is dedicated to the works of Francisco Salzillo, an 18th-century sculptor best known for his religious sculptures. It displays an extraordinary collection of his works, including the famous Holy Week processions.

Highlights

- Holy Week Sculptures: A collection of life-size polychrome wood sculptures representing scenes from the Passion of Christ.
- Nativity Scene: One of Spain's biggest and most intricate nativity scenes, including over 500 figurines.
- Exhibition Halls: Several halls displaying Salzillo's work and offering information about his life and creative process.

Practical information.

- Location: Plaza de San Agustín 3, 30005 Murcia.
- Opening hours are Tuesday through Saturday from 10:00 a.m. to 5:00 p.m. Sundays, 11 a.m. to 2 p.m. Closed on Mondays and holidays.
- Admission is around €5 for adults, with reductions for students and pensioners.
- Tips: To obtain a better appreciation of Salzillo's works, schedule your visit around the guided tours (available in different languages).

Santa Clara Monastery and Museum.

The Santa Clara Monastery, a tranquil monastery with a rich history reaching back to the 14th century, is home to the Santa Clara Museum, which displays a collection of religious art and antiques.

Highlights

- Islamic Art: A notable collection of Islamic pottery and antiquities from Murcia's Moorish history.
- Religious art includes beautiful altarpieces, sculptures, and paintings from many times.
- Architectural Features: The structure is a blend of Gothic and Baroque styles, with a tranquil courtyard that symbolizes its monastic origins.

- Location: Avenida Alfonso X El Sabio 1, 30008 Murcia.
- Tuesday through Saturday, 10:00 AM to 1:00 PM and 4:00 PM to 7:00 PM. Sundays and public holidays are from 11:00 a.m. to 1:00 p.m. Closed on Mondays.
- Admission: Free tip: Visit during the calmer afternoon hours to experience the peaceful environment. The museum is modest, so an hour or two is plenty for a complete tour.

Romea Theater.

The Romea Theatre, named for actor Julián Romea, is a cultural treasure in Murcia. Since its inception in 1862, it has held a number of theater  performances, concerts, and cultural gatherings.

Highlights

- Historic Architecture: The theater's architecture is reminiscent of 19th-century architectural styles, with a large façade and opulent interior.

- Cultural Events: A diversified calendar of events that includes plays, concerts, and dance performances with both local and foreign talent.
- Backstage Tours: These are sometimes offered and provide a view behind the scenes as well as information about the theater's history.

Practical information.

- Location: Plaza Julián Romea, 30001 Murcia
- The box office is open Monday through Friday from 9:00 AM to 2:00 PM and 5:00 PM to 8:00 PM. Performance schedules are available on the website or by contacting the theater.
- Admission: Ticket fees vary according to the event. Discounts are often provided to students, seniors, and organizations.
- Tip: Purchase tickets in advance, particularly for popular concerts. Arrive early to see the stunning building and have a drink at the theater's café.

Murcia's best attractions provide an intriguing blend of history, art, and culture. From the stately Murcia Cathedral and the sophisticated Real Casino de Murcia to the creative treasures of the Salzillo Museum, the calm Santa Clara Monastery, and the dynamic Romea Theatre, each location offers a distinct experience.

With the helpful information supplied, you can simply arrange your trips and make the most of your stay in this fascinating city.

Chapter 5: Cultural Experiences.

Murcia is a bustling area with a rich cultural past that provides a variety of activities for visitors. There's always something going on, from colorful festivals and fascinating flamenco concerts to engaging art galleries and busy local markets. This chapter will take you through the greatest cultural experiences Murcia has to offer, ensuring that you leave with lasting memories.

Festivals & Events.

Murcia has a number of festivals and events throughout the year, each highlighting the region's distinct customs and festive spirit. Here are several must-see festivities:

- *Semana Santa (Holy Week)*
- Semana Santa is a major religious holiday in Murcia. The city comes alive with processions that include magnificent floats, theatrical reenactments, and people dressed in traditional robes and hoods. The parade of "Salzillos," which are gorgeous sculptures made by the great Murcian artist Francisco Salzillo, is the highlight.
- Dates: Typically, in April (dates change annually according to the Easter calendar).
- Tips: Arrive early to have a good viewing place, particularly for large processions. Prepare for enormous crowds and a profoundly emotive event.

- *Bando de la Huerta.*
  This event honors Murcia's agricultural legacy with a colorful procession, traditional costumes, and folkloric music and dance. The city center is converted into a vibrant festival, complete with food kiosks serving regional delicacies.
- Dates: The Tuesday after Easter
- Tips: Wear comfortable shoes and be prepared to participate in the activities. Don't pass up the opportunity to sample the local cuisine and beverages offered at the food stand.

- Entierro de la Sardina (Burial of the Sardine).

This eccentric and boisterous celebration concludes Murcia's spring festivities. The major procession, which includes floats and music, culminates in the symbolic burning of a large sardine effigy, followed by fireworks.

- **Dates:** The Saturday after Easter Sunday.
- **Tips:** This is a family-friendly event, so bring the kids. Make sure to remain for the fireworks show that caps off the party.

- *Murcia Feria.*

The Murcia Feria is a week-long celebration with fairs, amusement rides, food vendors, and cultural events. The fairgrounds are alive with lights, music, and activities for all ages.

- **Dates:** early September.
- **Tips:** Visit in the evening when the fairgrounds are lit to experience the vivid atmosphere. Try some of the classic fair delicacies and ride the Ferris wheel for a spectacular perspective of the city.

- *Three Cultures International Festival.*

This celebration commemorates the historical cohabitation of Christians, Muslims, and Jews in Murcia. It includes a variety of cultural events such as music, dance, theater, and exhibits that celebrate the diversity and togetherness of diverse cultures.

- **Dates**: May.
- **Tips:** Check the event calendar ahead of time to arrange your visits to the most interesting performances and exhibits. The majority of activities are free for the general public.

Flamenco Shows in Murcia.

Flamenco, with its passionate music and dancing, is a vital element of Spanish culture, and Murcia has various places for experiencing this art form:

- *La Puerta Falsa.*

  La Puerta Falsa is a famous location for live music and flamenco performances. The compact environment provides an up-close view of the spectacular performances.
- **Location:** Calle San Martín de Porres 5, 30001 Murcia.
- **Tips:** Check the program in advance since performances fluctuate. Arrive early to get a nice seat and have a drink before the performance.

- *Café Del Archivo.*

  This beautiful café features frequent flamenco performances, offering an authentic and friendly setting in which to enjoy the music and dancing.
- **Location:** Calle Ceuta 8, 30007 Murcia.

- **Tip:** Reserve a table in advance, particularly on weekends. The café also serves an excellent assortment of tapas, ideal for a pre-show dinner.

Art Gallery and Exhibitions.

Murcia has a vibrant art scene, with galleries and institutions exhibiting both modern and traditional works:

- *Museo de Bellas Artes de Murcia (MUBAM).*

  MUBAM has an exceptional collection of Spanish art from the Middle Ages to the twentieth century. The museum's broad collection includes works by well-known painters including Murillo, Zurbarán, and Sorolla.
- **Location:** Calle Obispo Frutos 12, 30003 Murcia.
- **Admission is free,** making it an ideal low-cost activity. Plan on spending at least an hour examining the exhibits.

- *Centro Párraga.*

  This contemporary art center specializes in experimental and avant-garde art, including exhibits, performances, and workshops.
- **Location:** Calle Madre Elisea Oliver Molina 1, 30002 Murcia.

- **Tips:** Check the schedule for current exhibits and activities. This is an excellent site to see cutting-edge artwork and unique performances.

- *La conservera.*

  La Conservera, a contemporary art institution in Ceutí, showcases international and local artists via rotating exhibits. It is renowned for its inventive and thought-provoking installations.
- **Location:** Calle San Pedro 3, 30562 Ceutí, Murcia.
- **Tips:** Check their website for the most recent exhibition schedule. Spend a whole day exploring Ceutí's local attractions.

Traditional Crafts and Souvenirs.

Explore the region's traditional crafts and discover unique mementos to take home.

- *Esparto Grass Weaving.*

  Esparto grass weaving is a traditional craft in Murcia that produces baskets, mats, and ornamental pieces. You may discover these homemade things at local markets and specialized stores.

- **Where to Shop**: Mercado de Verónicas and artisan stores in the city center.
- **Tips:** Look for one-of-a-kind products like woven sandals or artistic wall hangings that would make excellent mementos or presents.

- *Ceramics.*
  Murcia is famous for its magnificent ceramics, which frequently have elaborate patterns and brilliant hues. These pieces make excellent decorative objects or functional cookware.
- **Where to Buy:** Local ceramic stores and the artisan area of the Mercado de Verónicas.
- **Tips:** Pack ceramic goods carefully to avoid breakage during transportation. Smaller things, such as tiles or plates, are more easily transported.

- *Embroidery, Lace*
  Murcia's ancient crafts include handcrafted embroidery and lace, which are often utilized in clothes, table linens, and ornamental objects. These beautiful items showcase the region's artisanal abilities.
- **Where to Buy:** Artisan stores in the city core and neighborhood markets.

- **Tips:** Look for products with typical Murcian motifs and patterns. These are great, lightweight presents that are simple to transport.

Local Markets in Murcia.

Exploring local markets is an excellent opportunity to see Murcia's everyday life while also finding fresh vegetables, local cuisines, and unique products:

- *Mercado de Verónicas*

  This lively market is the core of Murcia's gastronomic scene, with a diverse selection of fresh fruits, vegetables, meats, cheeses, and seafood. It's an excellent opportunity to taste local products and purchase items for a picnic or home-cooked supper.

- **Location:** Calle Verónicas 1, 30004 Murcia.

- **Opening hours** are Monday through Saturday from 8:00 a.m. to 2:30 p.m.

- **Tips:** Go to the market in the morning when it is most lively. Don't be afraid to test samples and ask the merchants for advice.

- *Mercado de San Agustín.*

  A contemporary market with a variety of vendors providing fresh vegetables, gourmet meals, and handcrafted goods. It also has various food kiosks where you can have freshly cooked meals.

- **Location:** Plaza de San Agustín 3, 30005 Murcia.
- **Opening hours** are Monday through Saturday from 8:00 a.m. to 2:30 p.m.
- **Tips:** This market is ideal for lunch, since many vendors have ready-to-eat alternatives. Try some of the local delicacies, such as "zarangollo" and "paparajotes."

- *El Zoco del Guadalabiad.*
  This flea market, held every Sunday in the La Flota district, sells a variety of antiques, secondhand items, and artisan crafts. It's a terrific spot to discover unusual goods and soak up the local market vibe.
- **Location:** Calle Pintor Pedro Cano, 30009 Murcia.
- **Opening hours:** Sundays, 9:00 a.m. to 2:00 p.m.
- **Tips:** Arrive early to have the finest choices. Bring cash, since some businesses may not take credit cards.

Murcia's cultural experiences are diverse and interesting, with something for everyone. From lively festivals and emotional flamenco concerts to stunning art galleries, traditional crafts, and busy markets, you'll have plenty of options to immerse yourself in local culture. Plan your trip around these activities to properly enjoy the region's beauty and energy.

Chapter 6: Day Trips & Excursions.

Murcia serves as an excellent base for exploring the neighboring locations, each of which has its own set of attractions and experiences. From ancient cities and beach getaways to natural parks and picturesque valleys, there's a lot to see and do in Murcia. This chapter will walk you through the top day trips and excursions, giving you practical information and ideas to help you make the most of your visit.

Cartagena.

Cartagena, a historic port city with more than 2,000 years of history, is a must-see trip. Cartagena, renowned for its rich cultural legacy and spectacular archaeological sites, provides an intriguing peek into Spain's past.

- *Roman Theatre.*

   The Roman Theatre is one of Cartagena's most famous landmarks. This well-preserved theater from the first century BC, discovered in the late twentieth century, provides a fascinating glimpse into Roman architecture and culture.

- **Tips:** Visit the Roman Theatre Museum to have a thorough grasp of the site's history and significance. The museum ticket also grants entry to the theater itself.

- **Cartagena Port and Promenade.**

   The busy port area is ideal for a leisurely stroll. The promenade showcases a combination of modern and antique structures, including the spectacular city hall and the Naval Museum.

- **Tips:** Take a boat tour of the harbor to get a fresh view of the city and its fortifications. Eat fresh seafood at one of the many seaside restaurants.

- *Concepcion Castle.*

Concepción Castle, located on a hill overlooking the city, provides panoramic views of Cartagena and its surroundings. The castle, which dates back to the Middle Ages, currently houses the History and Archaeology Museum.

- **Tips:** The climb to the castle can be difficult, but a lift is provided from the city center. Plan to spend a few hours exploring the museum and castle grounds.

La Manga del Mar Menor.

La Manga del Mar Menor is a distinctive coastal strip that separates the Mar Menor lagoon from the Mediterranean Sea. It is a popular resort for beachgoers and water sports aficionados.

- *Beaches of La Manga*

  La Manga has many magnificent beaches on both the Mediterranean and Mar Menor sides. The calm, shallow waters of the Mar Menor are ideal for families with young children.

- Playa de los Alemanes and Playa Paraíso are highly regarded for their cleanliness and amenities. Arrive early to ensure a nice place, particularly during high season.

- ***Water sports.***

  The tranquil seas of the Mar Menor make it perfect for water sports including windsurfing, kitesurfing, sailing, and kayaking. Several schools and rental stores cater to both beginners and expert aficionados.
- **Tip:** Schedule courses or equipment rentals ahead of time, especially during the summer. The optimum time for water sports is in the morning, when the winds are typically calmer.

- ***Natural parks.***
  Several natural parks around La Manga, notably Calblanque Regional Park, which is well-known for its unspoiled beaches, dunes, and hiking paths.
- **Tips:** when visiting Calblanque, bring plenty of water and sunscreen because the amenities are limited. The park is ideal for trekking and natural walks.

Sierra Espuña.

Sierra Espuña Regional Park is a natural sanctuary that offers a multitude of outdoor activities in gorgeous alpine landscapes. It's an excellent choice for nature lovers and adventure seekers.

- *Hikes and Nature Trails*
  Sierra Espuña offers hiking trails for all levels, including easy hikes and strenuous climbs. The park is home to a variety of flora and fauna, making it an ideal location for nature observation.
- **Tips:** Wear good hiking boots and bring a map or GPS device because certain trails are difficult to follow. Check the weather before you go, as the area is prone to rapid shifts.

- *Barracos de Gabe's.*

This spectacular terrain of eroding badlands is one of the park's most notable characteristics. The area has various vistas and paths that offer beautiful views of the distinctive environment.

- **Tips:** The best time to visit is in the early morning or late afternoon, when the light highlights the natural beauty of the terrain. Bring plenty of water and a camera to capture the breathtaking views.

- ***Snow wells (Pozos de Nieve).***
  These historic constructions were used to store snow and ice for later use in warmer months. The wells are an interesting monument to the region's ancient ice preservation techniques.

- The Snow Well Route is a popular trail that explores the intriguing history of Sierra Espuña. The terrain is quite tough, so be prepared to hike uphill.

Ricote Valley.

Ricote Valley is a lovely area recognized for its lush landscapes, quaint villages, and historical attractions. It provides a tranquil retreat from the hustle and bustle of the metropolis.

- *Villages in Ricote Valley.*

  The valley is populated with little communities including Ricote, Abarán, and Blanca. Each village has its own distinct appeal, complete with small streets, traditional buildings, and welcoming residents.

- **Tips:** Take some time to explore each community, sample local cuisine, and see historical places. Abarán is famed for its waterwheels, but Blanca has stunning river views.

- *Rio Segura.*

  The Segura River flows through the Ricote Valley, offering chances for kayaking, canoeing, and fishing. The riverbanks are ideal for picnics and leisurely hikes.

- **Tips:** Guided kayaking tours are available, providing a unique view of the valley. Pack a picnic and spend a relaxed day by the river.

- *La Navela's Viewpoint.*

  Hiking up to La Navela Viewpoint provides amazing panoramic views of the Ricote Valley. The ascent is quite difficult but well worth it for the breathtaking views.

- **Tips:** Pack water, food, and a camera. To avoid the midday heat, visit the viewpoint early in the morning or late afternoon.

Lorca.

Lorca is a medieval city famed for its majestic castle, rich cultural legacy, and lively festivals. It's a must-see for history and architecture buffs.

- ***Lorca Castle (Fortaleza del Sol).***
  Lorca Castle, commonly known as the fortification of the Sun, is a large medieval fortification with stunning views of the city and surrounding countryside. The castle offers a variety of exhibitions and activities throughout the year.
- **Tips:** Spend at least a couple of hours exploring the castle and its grounds. Check the schedule for any special events or guided tours that may complement your visit.

- ***Museo Azul de Semana Santa (MASS).***
  This museum honors Lorca's famed Holy Week celebrations. It displays exquisite costumes, floats, and antiques used in

processions, offering an intriguing glimpse into the city's traditions.

- **Tips:** The museum is a must-see for everyone interested in Spanish religious and cultural heritage. Combine your visit with a stroll in the historic city center.

- *Plaza De España.*

  Lorca's center square is flanked by impressive ancient buildings such as the Town Hall and the Collegiate Church of San Patricio. It's an excellent spot to unwind and take in the local atmosphere.

- **Tips:** While people-watching in the area, stop by one of the surrounding cafés for a coffee or dinner. The neighborhood is especially appealing in the evening, when the structures are illuminated.

Chapter 7: Food and Drink in Murcia, Spain.

Murcia is a gourmet treat, with a diverse culinary scene that reflects the region's agricultural bounty and cultural influences. From classic delicacies to innovative cuisine, there's something for everyone. This chapter will take you through Murcia's gastronomic scene, giving crucial information for food lovers planning a visit.

Traditional Murcian Cuisine.

Murcian cuisine is distinguished by its use of fresh, locally obtained ingredients, which represent the region's agricultural past. The recipes are basic but savory, frequently using vegetables, fish, and meats in harmonic pairings.

Caldero Murciano.

This is a classic fishermen's dish cooked with rice, fish (usually grouper or monkfish), and a thick, saffron broth. It's cooked in a unique pot known as a  caldero, which gives the meal its name.

Caldero is typically served with a side of (garlic mayonnaise). For the most refreshing experience, have it at a coastal restaurant.

Zarangollo.

Zarangollo, a simple yet delicious meal prepared with scrambled eggs, zucchini, and onions, is a Murcian culinary staple. It is commonly served as a tapa or side dish.

Tips: Pair zarangollo with a slice of crusty bread. It combines nicely with a glass of local wine.

Michirones.

Michirones are fava beans cooked with ham, chorizo, and seasonings. This hearty dish is generally served during the cooler months.

Michirones are best savored as a tapa at a local pub, paired with a cool beer.

Pastel de carne.

This savory meat pie, prepared with a flaky pastry crust and filled with pork, beef, and eggs, is a popular snack in Murcia.

Tips: Look for pastel de carne in local bakeries or enjoy it as a quick snack while visiting the city.

The best restaurants and tapas bars in Murcia.

Murcia has a busy dining scene, ranging from upscale restaurants to modest tapas bars. Here are some must-see venues to sample the best of Murcian cuisine.

- *La Petite Taberna.*

La Pequeña Taberna, located in the heart of Murcia, offers traditional meals and a welcoming ambiance. The menu includes a range of Murcian dishes.

- **Tip:** Make a reservation, particularly on weekends. Do not miss the zarangollo and octopus dishes.

- *El Pasaje de Zabalburu*

  This popular tapas bar serves a diverse selection of contemporary and traditional tapas. The bustling atmosphere makes it an excellent place to begin an evening out.

- **Tip:** Try the marinated anchovies and croquettes. Arrive early as it can become packed.

- Restaurante Salzillo.

  Restaurante Salzillo, known for its attractive atmosphere and high-quality cuisine, provides a sophisticated dining experience centered on regional cuisines.

- **Tips:** A tasting menu is an excellent way to try a range of foods. To really enjoy your dinner, pair it with a local wine.

- *La tapa.*

  La Tapa, located near the cathedral, is well-known for its vast menu of superb tapas. It's the ideal place for a relaxed supper with friends.

- **Tip:** Order a selection of tapas for sharing. Their jamón ibérico and patatas bravas come highly recommended.

Murcia Wine and Vineyards.

Murcia is located in Spain's southern wine area and is well-known for its diverse wine production. The region's climate and geography are perfect for growing a wide range of grape varieties.

- **Jumilla**.

  Jumilla, one of Murcia's most famous wine-producing regions, is noted for its strong red wines created predominantly from the Monastrell grape variety.
- **Tips:** Take a tour and taste at one of Jumilla's many wineries. Bodegas Luzón and Casa Castillo are popular options.

- *Bullas*.

The Bullas wine region is known for its high-quality red, white, and rosé wines. The area also has a wine museum, which provides information about the region's vineyards.

- **Tips:** The Bullas Wine Museum is an excellent starting point for exploring the nearby wineries. Bodegas del Rosario and Bodega Monastrell are worth seeing.

- *Yecla.*
  Yecla is another renowned wine-producing region known for its Monastrell-based wines. The region's vineyards benefit from its high altitude and Mediterranean environment.

- **Tips:** Combine a wine tour with a visit to the picturesque town of Yecla. Bodegas Castaño and Barahonda provide excellent tours and tastings.

Cooking Classes and Food Tours.

Take a cooking class or go on a food tour to get a taste of Murcia's cuisine. These events provide hands-on opportunity to learn about local foods and cooking methods.

- *Murcia Cooking Experience.*
  This famous cooking school teaches students how to produce traditional Murcian cuisine with fresh, local ingredients. Classes are taught by expert chefs.

- **Tip:** Make sure to book your lesson ahead of time. The paella and caldero lessons are especially popular.

- *Murcia Tapas Tour.*
  Join a guided tapas tour to discover Murcia's greatest tapas bars. You'll visit numerous restaurants and sample a range of tapas and local wines along the route.
- **Tips:** Wear comfortable shoes and bring an appetite. The tour is a fantastic opportunity to discover the city's culinary culture while meeting other foodies.

- *Wine and Olive Oil Tasting.*
  Combine your love for wine and olive oil with a tasting tour that visits local wineries and olive oil producers. Learn about the manufacturing procedures and enjoy sampling.
- **Tip:** These excursions frequently include a lunch or tapas pairing, so plan accordingly. Look for packages that include transportation to and from Murcia City.

Local Markets and Street Food.

Murcia's markets are a foodie's dream, featuring a diverse selection of fresh vegetables, local delicacies, and street cuisine. Visiting these markets is an excellent opportunity to learn about local culture and flavors.

- *Verónica's Market*

  This lively market is Murcia's largest, with a diverse assortment of fresh fruits, vegetables, meats, seafood, and more. It's an excellent spot to discover the region's culinary diversity.

- Visit in the morning, when the market is at its busiest. Don't miss the seafood sellers and the opportunity to sample freshly prepared tapas.

- *Plaza de la Flores.*

  This vibrant square is flanked by flower stalls and tapas bars, making it a popular destination for both locals and visitors. It's an excellent area to have a leisurely dinner or snack.

- **Tips**: Try the local marineras (anchovies in a Russian salad base) and pasteles de carne. The atmosphere is especially lively at night.

- *Street Food Festivals.*

  Murcia holds various street food events throughout the year, where you may try a wide range of local and international cuisine. These festivals provide an excellent opportunity to sample the city's dynamic cuisine culture.

- **Tips:** Check your local listings for upcoming festivals. Some sellers may not accept credit cards, so bring cash. Arrive early to prevent long waits.

Chapter 8: Shopping in Murcia.

Murcia provides a diversified shopping experience by combining ancient markets and artisan stores with modern malls and business districts. Whether you're seeking unusual souvenirs, high-end apparel, or vintage treasures, there are plenty of possibilities to meet your shopping needs. This chapter will show you the best shopping districts, boutiques, malls, and marketplaces in Murcia.

Shopping districts.

Murcia's shopping areas are dynamic hubs with a mix of local businesses, worldwide brands, and unique boutiques. Here are some of the main locations to investigate:

- *Gran Vía Escultor Francisco Salzillo.*

  The Gran Vía, Murcia's main shopping artery, features a diverse range of stores, including high-end designer boutiques and popular multinational chains.
- **Location:** Central Murcia, beginning near the Plaza de Santo Domingo and extending to the river.
- **Tips:** The Gran Vía offers cafes and eateries for a relaxing break and people-watching experience.

- *Platería & Trapería streets.*

  These two parallel alleys are some of Murcia's oldest and most picturesque shopping sections. They have a mix of traditional businesses, jewelry stores, and artisanal boutiques.
- **Location:** In the old center, near Murcia Cathedral.
- **Tips:** Stop by the little shops selling homemade crafts and jewelry. The area is pedestrian-friendly, making it perfect for a leisurely retail stroll.

- *Alfonso X El Sabio Avenue.*

  This boulevard is notable for its wide walkways and diverse shops, which include clothes boutiques, bookstores, and cafes. It's a busy location that attracts both locals and tourists.
- **Location:** Parallel to Gran Vía, near Plaza Circular.
- Don't overlook the local bookstores and gourmet shops. The avenue is attractively lit in the nights, creating a welcoming retail environment.

Local boutiques and artisan shops.

Murcia's boutiques and artisan shops are filled with one-of-a-kind and locally manufactured products. Here are some must-see spots:

- *Artesania de Murcia.*

  This business specializes in local crafts and sells a wide variety of handmade things such as ceramics, textiles, and jewelry. It's an excellent spot to find original Murcian items.
- **Location:** Calle Calderón de la Barca, 4.
- **Tips:** Take your time looking through the many categories and learning about the various crafts. The personnel is typically competent and may offer insights about the products.

- *La Tiendavde Las Flores.*

This beautiful boutique sells a wide range of floral-themed items, from fresh flowers to decorative pieces and accessories. It's an excellent spot to look for unique gifts.

- **Location:** Plaza de las Flores.
- **Tips:** Make a stop at one of the surrounding cafes for a great shopping experience. The region is bustling and full of character.

- *Merca- Rincón del Artesania.*
  This business, a cooperative of local craftsmen, sells a variety of handcrafted goods such as leatherwork, pottery, and wood carvings. Each piece is created with care and attention to detail.
- **Location:** Calle Frenería, 6.
- **Tips:** Look for on-site workshops where you can observe craftsmen work and perhaps join in crafting sessions.

Murcia Malls and Commercial Centers.

Murcia's malls and commercial centers offer a pleasant shopping experience with a diverse selection of stores under one roof. Here are a few of the top destinations:

- *Centro Comercial Nueva Condomina.*

This enormous retail mall has approximately 200 stores, including fashion boutiques, technology stores, and a variety of restaurants. It also includes a cinema and recreational area.

- **Location:** Autovía A-7, Salidas 760, Murcia.
- **Tips:** Check the mall's website for details on sales and activities. There's plenty to see and do here, so plan on spending several hours.

- ***Thader Shopping Center.***
  Thader is another popular shopping area with a variety of retail businesses, restaurants, and entertainment options. It is well-known for its modern style and roomy layout.
- **Address**: Avenida Juan de Borbón, Murcia.
- **Tips:** Visit during the week to escape the weekend crowds. Keep an eye out for the center's unique events and promotions.

- ***El corte inglès.***
  Spain's well-known department store company has a huge location in Murcia, selling everything from fashion and beauty products to home furnishings and gourmet food.
- **Location:** Avenida de la Libertad, Murcia.
- El Corte Inglés is an excellent destination for one-stop shopping. The store's customer service is exceptional, and they frequently offer exclusive products and brands.

Flea Markets and Vintage Finds.

For those who love hunting for unique items and bargains, Murcia's flea markets and vintage shops are a must-visit. These spots offer a mix of antiques, collectibles, and second-hand treasures.

- Mercado de La Fama

  This popular flea market is held every Sunday and features a wide variety of stalls selling antiques, vintage clothing, books, and more.
- **Location:** Avenida de La Fama, Murcia.
- **Tips:** Arrive early for the best selection of items. Bring cash, as many vendors may not accept credit cards. Be prepared to haggle for better prices.

- *Rastro de Murcia.*

  Held on Saturday mornings, this market is known for its eclectic mix of second-hand goods, from furniture and home decor to clothing and accessories.
- **Location:** Barrio del Carmen, near the train station.
- **Tips:** Wear comfortable shoes, as the market covers a large area. It's a great place to find unique and affordable items.

- ***Retroklang.***

  A vintage shop specializing in clothing and accessories from past decades, Retroklang is a favorite among fashion enthusiasts and collectors.
- **Location:** Calle Acisclo Díaz, 4, Murcia.
- **Tips:** Check their social media for updates on new arrivals and special sales. The shop also offers styling advice and customization services.

Chapter 9: Nightlife and Entertainment in Murcia Spain.

Murcia comes alive after dark, with a dynamic nightlife and a variety of entertainment alternatives. Murcia has something for everyone, whether you want to drink drinks in a trendy bar, dance the night away in a nightclub, listen to live music, or see a production in the theater. This chapter will show you the greatest places to enjoy Murcia's nightlife and entertainment scene.

Murcia Best Bars and Pubs.

Murcia has a diverse range of bars and pubs, from upscale cocktail lounges to intimate local taverns. Here are some of the best venues to grab a drink.

- *La Consentida.*

La Consentida is a chic cocktail bar recognized for its inventive concoctions and sophisticated setting. The bartenders are expert mixologists who can create both classic and inventive cocktails.

- **Address:** Calle de la Princesa 18, Murcia.
- **Tips:** Try their signature cocktails, which frequently use local ingredients. The pub is busy on weekends, so arrive early to secure a nice seat.

- *Sala Revolver.*

  Sala Revolver, a favorite neighborhood hangout, provides a casual ambiance and a diverse assortment of beers, including numerous craft alternatives. The decor is eclectic, and there's usually live music or DJ sets.
- **Address:** Calle Victorio 19, Murcia.
- Check the schedule for live music nights. The outside seating area is ideal for enjoying Murcia's warm nights.

- *Bar Ficciones.*

  This quirky pub is popular among students and young professionals. Bar Ficciones is noted for its relaxed atmosphere, affordable beverages, and regular cultural activities such as poetry readings and indie cinema screenings.
- **Address:** Calle Fuensanta 5, Murcia.

- **Tip:** Don't miss their themed nights, which frequently include special cocktails and entertainment. It's an excellent spot to meet people and explore Murcia's creative culture.

Nightclubs and Dance Venues in Murcia.

Murcia's nightclubs and dance venues provide a variety of experiences, including high-energy dance floors and more private settings. Here are some of the top spots to dance your night away:

- *Musik.*

  Musik is one of Murcia's most popular nightclubs, with three dance floors, a rooftop terrace, and a mix of local and foreign DJs. Music genres include electronic and house, as well as hip-hop and Latin sounds.
- **Address:** Calle de La Aurora 1, Murcia.
- **Tip:** For the finest vibe, arrive after midnight. Dress to impress, as the club boasts a stylish, affluent atmosphere.

- *Boutique Club.*

  This elite club provides a magnificent nightlife experience with its attractive decor, VIP rooms, and high-quality sound system. Boutique Club is recognized for its special events and theme nights.
- **Address:** Avenida Ciclista Mariano Rojas 2, Murcia.

- **Tip:** Make reservations for a table or VIP section in advance, especially on weekends. The club frequently hosts guest DJs and live performances.

- *Garaje Beat Club.*
  Garaje Beat Club offers a more alternative evening experience. This club features live bands, DJ evenings, and themed events, with a focus on indie, rock, and electronic genres.
- **Address:** Avenida Miguel de Cervantes 45, Murcia.
- Check the event calendar for upcoming concerts and themed nights. Casual clothes are acceptable at the club due to its relaxed dress code.

Live Music and Performance.

Murcia has a robust live music culture, with venues hosting everything from jazz and blues to rock and classical concerts. Here are some of the best places to see live music.

- *Teatro Circo Murcia.*
  This historic theater provides a variety of performances, including live music, theater, and dance. The theater itself is stunning, with elaborate architecture and great acoustics.
- **Address:** Calle Enrique Villar 11, Murcia.

- **Tips:** Check the schedule ahead of time and get tickets early, since popular shows often sell out quickly. The theater also provides guided tours of the ancient edifice.

- *Sala REM.*
- Sala REM is a diverse facility that showcases both local and international musicians, making it a popular destination for live music enthusiasts. The facility regularly hosts club nights featuring a variety of musical styles.
- **Address:** Calle Puerta Nueva 33, Murcia.
- **Tips:** Arrive early to get a good view of the stage. The venue provides a relaxing environment and frequently offers beer discounts.

- *Jazzazza Jazz Club.*

  Jazzazza Jazz Club is an excellent choice for a more intimate live music experience. This intimate club hosts live jazz performances in a relaxing and inviting atmosphere.
- **Address:** Avenida Juan Carlos I, 4 Algezares, Murcia.
- **Tip:** Make reservations, especially on weekends. The club also serves tapas and cocktails, making it an ideal destination for a night out.

Murcia Murcia's Theaters and Cinemas.

Murcia's theaters and cinemas provide a variety of cultural and leisure experiences, including classic plays, new performances, and the latest films.

- *Teatro Romea.*

  Teatro Romea, one of Murcia's most prominent theaters, hosts a wide range of acts, including plays, operas, and concerts. The theater's great grandeur and historical significance enhance the experience.
- **Location:** Plaza Julián Romea, Murcia.
- **Tips:** Check the performance schedule and reserve tickets ahead of time. The theater's central location makes it convenient to combine with a meal or drinks in the surrounding region.

- *Filmoteca Regional Francisco Rabal.*

  This regional film archive and cinema screens classic films, independent films, and worldwide cinema. It's an excellent spot to see a unique film that you won't see in mainstream theaters.
- **Location:** Avenida de la Libertad 1, Murcia.

- **Tip:** Look for themed film series and unique activities. The cinema frequently offers Q&A sessions with filmmakers and actors.
- *Cine Rex.*

  Cine Rex, a prominent cinema in the heart of Murcia, shows both blockbuster and independent films. The contemporary facilities and comfy seating improve the moviegoing experience.
- **Location:** Calle Concepción 7, Murcia.
- **Tip:** Book your tickets online to avoid long lineups, especially on weekends. The cinema also has a loyalty program for frequent moviegoers.

Casinos & Gaming

Murcia offers various casinos and gaming locations that offer a variety of gambling opportunities, including slot machines and poker tables.

- *Gran Casino Murcia.*

  This casino, housed in the ancient Real Casino de Murcia structure, blends magnificent architecture with modern gaming amenities. It provides a variety of games, such as roulette, blackjack, and poker.
- **Address:** Calle Trapería 18, Murcia.

- **Tips:** The dress code is smart casual. The casino also has a restaurant and a bar, making it an excellent choice for a full night out.

- ***Orenes Gran Casino, Murcia Rincón de Pepe.***
  This casino is another great gaming destination with a diverse assortment of gaming options, including slot machines and live table games. The attractive decor and expert staff provide a premium feel.
- *Address:* Calle Apóstoles 34, Murcia.
- Check for special offers and contests. For added convenience, consider staying in the Hotel Rincón de Pepe, which also houses the casino.

- ***Bingo Roma.***
  Bingo Roma provides a more relaxed gaming experience by hosting bingo games in a lively, sociable environment. It's a pleasant way to spend the evening and possibly win some rewards.
- **Location:** Calle Floridablanca 3, Murcia.
- **Tips:** Arrive early to ensure a decent seat. The location also sells snacks and drinks, making it a pleasant place to spend a couple of hours.

Chapter 10: Family-Friendly Activities in Murcia Spain.

Murcia is an excellent family destination, with a wide range of activities suitable for both children and adults. This chapter will walk you through the greatest family-friendly activities in Murcia, including interactive museums and lively parks, as well as kid-friendly attractions and food alternatives.

Kid-friendly attractions

Murcia has a variety of attractions that are ideal for families with children, providing both fun and educational opportunities.

- **_Terra Natura Murcia._**

    Terra Natura is a combined wildlife and water park. The zoo houses approximately 300 animals from throughout the world, while the water park has slides, pools, and water play areas.

- **Location:** Cañada del Gallego, s/n, 30100 Espinardo, Murcia.
- **Tips:** Allow for a full day to explore both the zoo and the water park. Bring swimsuits, sunscreen, and hats to the water park, and wear comfortable shoes when wandering around the zoo.

- *Museo de la Ciencia y el Agua.*
  The Science and Water Museum is an interactive museum where children may participate in hands-on displays about science, technology, and the environment. There is also a planetarium for stargazing shows.
- **Location:** Plaza de la Ciencia, 1; 30002 Murcia.
- Check the museum's schedule for special seminars and exhibitions. The planetarium performances are especially popular with children, so purchase tickets in advance if possible.

- *Aqua Natura.*
  Aqua Natura is a water park located next to Terra Natura. It has a wave pool, slides, a lazy river, and areas intended exclusively for small children.
- *Location:* Terra Natura Murcia.

- **Tips:** For a complete day of enjoyment, visit both Aqua Natura and Terra Natura. Bring towels, and consider hiring a locker to keep your valuables.

Parks and playgrounds in Murcia.

Murcia's parks and playgrounds are ideal places for kids to play, explore, and burn off energy.

- *Jardin de Floridablanca.*

   This ancient park in the city center is Murcia's oldest public garden. It has shady walks, lovely flower beds, and a spacious playground area for kids.
- **Location:** Calle Proclamación 6, 30002 Murcia.
- **Tips:** This park is ideal for a family picnic or a leisurely stroll. The playground is well-maintained and appropriate for children of all ages.

- *Parque de la Seda.*

   A big urban park with numerous green spaces, playgrounds, and walking pathways. It also has a lake where families can hire paddle boats.
- **Location:** Avenida Intendente Jorge Palacios, Murcia.

- **Tips:** Bring a ball or a frisbee for the open grass sections. There are various cafes and booths throughout the park that serve food and refreshments.

- *Parque Infantile de Trafico.*
  This unique park is intended to teach children about driving rules and road safety. It has little roads, traffic lights, and small automobiles for children to ride.
- **Location:** Calle de Juan Carlos I, 10, Murcia.
- **Tips:** It's a fun and instructive activity for kids. The park is open on weekends and holidays, so check the schedule before you go.

Family-friendly restaurants.

Family-friendly restaurants In Murcia, it is simple to find a restaurant that caters to both children and adults. Below are some family-friendly dining options:

- *Restaurante La Tapa.*
  La Tapa serves tapas and traditional Spanish meals in a casual, family-friendly setting. The menu includes selections for both children and adults.
- **Address:** Plaza de las Flores 8, 30004 Murcia.

- **Tip:** The outside seating area is ideal for families, allowing children to move freely. Try their house-made tapas, which are popular among both residents and tourists.

- *Pizzeria La Mafia SE Sienta a la Mesa.*
  This Italian restaurant is well-known for its wonderful pizzas and pasta dishes. The relaxing atmosphere and courteous staff make it ideal for families.
- **Location:** Calle Alejandro Seiquer 4, 30001 Murcia.
- **Tips:** The restaurant has a separate kids' menu and frequently gives coloring books and crayons to keep children entertained.

- *La Mary Restaurant.*
  La Mary has a warm atmosphere and a broad menu that caters to both adults and children. They offer Mediterranean cuisine with a modern flare.
- **Location:** Calle Cánovas del Castillo 6, 30003 Murcia.
- **Tips:** The restaurant's central position makes it an ideal spot for a family supper while exploring the city. Reservations are essential, particularly on weekends.

Murcia's Zoos and Aquariums

Murcia's zoos and aquariums provide excellent possibilities for children to learn about animals and aquatic life.

- *Terra Natura Murcia.*

  As previously said, Terra Natura is a wildlife park that houses creatures from all over the world. It focuses on conservation and education, making it an excellent learning opportunity for children.

- **Location:** Cañada del Gallego, s/n, 30100 Espinardo, Murcia.

- **Tips:** Attend planned animal feedings and talks to get a better look at the animals and learn about their surroundings.

- *Aquarium at the University of Murcia.*

  This small yet instructive aquarium, part of the University of Murcia, displays a variety of marine animals. It's an excellent spot for children to learn about marine life.

- **Location:** Campus de Espinardo, Murcia (30100).

- **Tips:** The aquarium is part of the university's research endeavors, therefore educational tours and seminars are frequently available. Call ahead to learn about any special activities or tours.

Educational Tours & Museums.

Murcia offers a plethora of museums and educational trips that are both entertaining and enlightening for youngsters.

- *Museo Salzillo.*

  This museum is dedicated to the works of the famed Baroque sculptor Francisco Salzillo and offers guided tours that can be modified for children. The elaborate statues are intriguing and offer insight into Spain's creative legacy.

- **Location:** Plaza de San Agustín 3, 30005 Murcia.

- **Tips:** Look for family-friendly tours and activities that will make the museum experience more interesting for young visitors.

- *Museo de la Ciudad.*

  The City Museum of Murcia offers an interactive tour through Murcia's history, from antiquity to the present. It's an excellent opportunity for children to learn about local culture and history.

- **Location:** Plaza Agustinas 7, 30005 Murcia.

- **Tip:** The museum frequently features unique exhibits and hands-on activities for youngsters. Check out their website for information on current events and programming.

- *Educational Tours.*

  Several groups in Murcia provide educational excursions suitable for families. These trips might include everything from historical walks through the city to wildlife excursions in local parks and reserves.

- Consider organizing a guided tour focused on your children's interests, such as history, nature, or art. Many tours are intended to be interactive and entertaining for younger people.

Chapter 11: Murcia Seasonal Guide.

Murcia is a year-round destination, offering something unique and exciting in every season. Understanding the best times to visit, the local weather, and the special events throughout the year can help you plan your trip more effectively. This chapter will guide you through the seasonal highlights of Murcia.

Best Times to Visit

Murcia has a Mediterranean climate, making it pleasant to visit almost any time of the year. However, the best times to visit depend on your interests and what you hope to experience.

- *Spring (March to May).*

Spring is one of the best times to visit Murcia, with mild temperatures, blooming flowers, and fewer tourists. It's perfect for outdoor activities and sightseeing.

- **Highlights:** Enjoy the lush landscapes, participate in local festivals, and explore Murcia's parks and gardens in full bloom.

- *Summer (June to August).*

Summer is hot and sunny, ideal for beachgoers and those looking to enjoy coastal activities. However, it can be quite hot inland, so plan accordingly.

- **Highlights:** Head to the beaches of La Manga del Mar Menor, enjoy water sports, and experience the vibrant nightlife.

- *Autumn (September to November).*
Autumn offers warm temperatures and a slightly quieter tourist scene. It's a great time for cultural experiences and exploring the countryside.

- **Highlights:** Harvest festivals, wine tasting, and pleasant weather for hiking and nature trails.

- *Winter (December to February).*
Winter is mild, making it suitable for sightseeing and enjoying the city's cultural attractions. While it's not beach weather, the

temperate climate is perfect for exploring Murcia's historical sites.

- **Highlights:** Festive events, fewer crowds, and comfortable weather for city tours and museum visits.

Weather and Climate.

Understanding Murcia's climate can help you prepare for your trip. Here's a breakdown of the typical weather you can expect each season.

Spring

- Temperature: 15°C to 25°C (59°F to 77°F)
- Weather: Mild and pleasant, occasional rain showers.

Summer.

- Temperature: 25°C to 35°C (77°F to 95°F)
- Weather: Hot and dry, perfect for beach activities.

Autumn.

- Temperature: 17°C to 28°C (63°F to 82°F)
- Weather: Warm and comfortable, with occasional rain.

Winter.

- Temperature: 10°C to 18°C (50°F to 64°F)

- Weather: Mild and mostly dry, ideal for exploring the city.

Seasonal Events and Festivals.

Murcia hosts a variety of events and festivals throughout the year. Here are some highlights to consider when planning your visit:

Spring.

Semana Santa (Holy Week).

- Date: Varies (March or April)
- Overview: Celebrated with elaborate processions, traditional music, and religious ceremonies. It's one of the most important events in Murcia's cultural calendar.

Bando de la Huerta.

- Date: Tuesday after Easter
- Overview: A lively festival celebrating Murcia's agricultural heritage with traditional costumes, parades, and local food.
- Summer

Festival Internacional de Folklore en el Mediterráneo.

- Date: Early July
- Overview: An international folklore festival featuring music, dance, and cultural performances from around the world.

Cante de las Minas.

- Date: August
- Overview: One of Spain's most prestigious flamenco festivals, held in the nearby town of La Unión. It's a must-see for flamenco enthusiasts.

Autumn.

Fiestas de Otoño (Autumn Festivals).

- Date: September
- Overview: A series of events including the Feria de Murcia, with concerts, fairground attractions, and street performances.

Entierro de la Sardina.

- Date: First weekend after Easter
- Overview: A quirky and fun festival marking the end of the Spring festivities with a symbolic "burial of the sardine," fireworks, and parades.

Winter.

Navidad (Christmas).

- Date: December 24th to January 6th
- Overview: Christmas markets, nativity scenes, and festive lights create a magical atmosphere in Murcia. The celebrations culminate with the Three Kings Parade on January 5th.

Festival de los Reyes Magos (Three Kings Festival).

- Date: January 5th
- Overview: A festive parade celebrating the arrival of the Three Wise Men, with floats, music, and sweets for children.

Packing Tips for Each Season

To make the most of your visit, it's essential to pack appropriately for the season. Here are some tips on what to bring:

Spring.

- Clothing: Light layers, a mix of short and long sleeves, a light jacket or sweater.
- Accessories: Comfortable walking shoes, sunglasses, and a hat.
- Other Essentials: An umbrella or raincoat for occasional showers.

Summer.

- Clothing: Lightweight, breathable fabrics, shorts, t-shirts, swimwear.
- Accessories: Sunblock, sunglasses, a wide-brimmed hat, and sandals.
- Other Essentials: Reusable water bottle, beach towel, and a small backpack for day trips.

Autumn.

- Clothing: Light layers, long sleeves, a mix of light and warm clothing.
- Accessories: Comfortable walking shoes, a light jacket or sweater for cooler evenings.
- Other Essentials: An umbrella or raincoat for occasional rain.

Winter.

- Clothing: Warm layers, including sweaters, long pants, and a medium-weight jacket.
- Accessories: Comfortable walking shoes, a scarf, and gloves for cooler days.
- Other Essentials: A travel guide or book for indoor activities during any unexpected cold or rainy days.

Chapter 12: Practical Tips.

Traveling to Murcia is an exciting adventure, and being well-prepared can help make the journey go smoothly. This chapter offers practical advice on internet and mobile connectivity, electricity and plug kinds, accessibility, tourist information centers, and helpful apps and services for travelers.

Internet and Mobile Connectivity.

Staying connected while traveling is critical for navigating, communicating, and getting information. Here is everything you need to know about internet and mobile access in Murcia.

Wi-Fi Availability.

- Hotels & accommodations: The majority of Murcia's hotels, hostels, and guesthouses provide free Wi-Fi to their customers. Check with your accommodation ahead of time to check availability and any potential charges.

- Many cafés, bars, and restaurants offer free Wi-Fi to its clients. Look for signage advertising free Wi-Fi, or ask the staff for the password.

- Murcia provides free Wi-Fi in select public spaces, including parks and plazas. The city also provides internet access in libraries and other governmental buildings.

Mobile connectivity.

- **SIM Cards:** If you want to use your phone frequently, consider getting a local SIM card. Major carriers such as Movistar, Vodafone, and Orange provide prepaid SIM cards with data bundles. These can be obtained at mobile phone stores, airports, and some convenience shops.
- **Roaming:** If you have an international plan with your home operator, look into the roaming fees and options accessible in Spain. Some businesses give economical European travel packages.

Electricity and Plug Types.

Understanding the local electrical standards and plug types will allow you to keep your devices charged and ready to use.

Electrical Standards.

- The standard voltage in Spain is 230 volts.
- Frequency: 50 Hz.

Plug Types:

- Plug Type C: Two round pins (common in Europe).
- Plug Type F: Two spherical pins with two earth clips on each side (common in Europe).

Travel Adapters.

- **Recommendation:** Bring a universal travel adaptor so that your devices can be plugged in. If you're carrying many gadgets, think about using a power strip with surge protection.
- **Accessibility Information:** Murcia is committed to make the city accessible to all visitors, especially people with disabilities. Here are some crucial points about accessibility in Murcia.

Public Transportation

- **Buses:** Many city buses have ramps and dedicated handicapped spots. They also make audio-visual announcements at stops.
- **Trains:** Major train stations are generally accessible, with elevators, ramps, and help services. It is recommended that you contact the station ahead of time to confirm any specific services.
- **Taxis:** Some taxi firms have accessible vehicles. It is recommended that you schedule ahead of time and explain your requirements.

Accommodations.

- Many hotels in Murcia have accessible rooms and facilities. Check the hotel's website or call them directly to confirm the availability of accessible rooms and services.
- Public Spaces: The city has taken steps to ensure that significant attractions, museums, and public buildings are accessible. Look for information on accessibility on official websites or contact the sites directly.

Assistance Services.

- Tourist Offices: Staff at tourist information centers can provide information about nearby attractions, services, and transportation.
- Tourist Information Centers: Murcia's tourist information centers are excellent tools for visitors. They provide maps, brochures, and tailored assistance to help you get the most out of your vacation.

Main Tourist Information Centers.

Murcia City Center Office.

- Location: Plaza Cardenal Belluga, Murcia.

- Services include maps, brochures, event information, hotel reservations, and guided tour information.
- Tips: The staff speaks several languages and can provide thorough information about the city and nearby areas.

Tourist Information Office in the Train Station.

- Location: Murcia del Carmen Train Station.
- Services include travel assistance, transportation information, maps, and brochures.
- Tips: Ideal for travelers arriving by rail. When you arrive, ask for recommendations for local transportation and sights.

Other Useful Information Centers.

- La Manga Tourism Office
- Location: Gran Vía de La Manga in San Javier.
- Services include information on beaches, activities, and accommodations in the La Manga area.

Apps and Resources for Travelers

- Using technology can improve your trip experience in Murcia. Here are some helpful applications and tools to have before your vacation.

Navigation and Transportation.

Google Maps is essential for getting around the city, discovering attractions, and checking public transportation routes and schedules.

Moovit: Offers thorough information about public transit, including real-time bus and rail schedules.

Language & Communication.

- Google Translate is useful for translating phrases and conversations. The program includes offline translation and a chat mode to facilitate communication.
- Duolingo: A fun method to practice basic Spanish phrases before or during your trip.

Travel Guides and Local Information.

- TripAdvisor: Get reviews and recommendations for restaurants, sights, and accommodations.
- Visit Murcia App: The official tourism app for Murcia, with information on sites, events, maps, and excursions.

Currency & Finance.

- XE Currency: Keeps you informed about currency exchange rates and assists with conversions.

- Revolut is a travel-friendly banking app that provides competitive currency rates and allows you to manage your money on the road.

Event and Activity Planning.

- **Eventbrite**: Discover local events, festivals, and activities taking place in Murcia during your visit.
- **Meetup:** Find local groups and events depending on your interests, which is an excellent way to meet locals and other visitors.

Using these useful suggestions and tools, you may improve your travel experience in Murcia, assuring a seamless, enjoyable, and well-connected trip.

Chapter 13: Murcia Itineraries.

Planning your trip to Murcia is easier with well-crafted itineraries tailored to different interests and lengths of stay. Here are some carefully curated itineraries to help you make the most of your time in Murcia, whether you have one day, a weekend, a week, or specific interests in food, wine, and family activities.

One Day in Murcia

Morning.

- Murcia Cathedral: Start your day at the stunning Murcia Cathedral. Take a guided tour to appreciate its Gothic architecture and the beautiful baroque facade. Don't miss climbing the tower for panoramic views of the city.

- Plaza Cardenal Belluga: Enjoy the lively atmosphere of the square and take in the sights of the Episcopal Palace and other historic buildings.

Late Morning.

- Real Casino de Murcia: Explore this elegant social club, known for its lavish interiors. The guided tour covers the library, ballroom, and other opulent rooms.

Lunch.

- Local Tapas Bar: Head to the city center and enjoy a traditional Murcian lunch at a local tapas bar. Try delicacies like marineras, zarangollo, and Murcia-style cod.

Afternoon.

- Salzillo Museum: Visit this museum dedicated to the works of Francisco Salzillo, a renowned Spanish Baroque sculptor. The intricately carved figures are a highlight.
- Santa Clara Monastery & Museum: Discover the history and art housed within this former convent. The peaceful gardens provide a pleasant break.

Evening.

- Romea Theatre: If you have time, check out the program at the historic Romea Theatre. Even if you don't see a performance, the building's architecture is worth admiring.
- Dinner at a Riverside Restaurant: End your day with dinner by the Segura River, enjoying regional dishes and a relaxing ambiance.

Weekend Getaway.

Day 1: Historical and Cultural Highlights.

- Morning: Start with the Murcia Cathedral and Plaza Cardenal Belluga.
- Late Morning: Real Casino de Murcia.
- Lunch: Enjoy tapas at a central restaurant.
- Afternoon: Salzillo Museum and Santa Clara Monastery & Museum.
- Evening: Stroll through the city center, followed by dinner at a traditional Spanish restaurant.

Day 2: Nature and Relaxation.

- Morning: Visit the Terra Natura Murcia, a zoo and water park that is fun for all ages.
- Lunch: Picnic in the park or lunch at the zoo's café.

- Afternoon: Head to the Floridablanca Garden for a leisurely walk.
- Evening: Relax with a spa treatment at a local wellness center, then dine at a riverside restaurant.

One Week in Murcia.

Day 1-2: Explore the City

- Day 1: Follow the one-day itinerary.
- Day 2: Discover Murcia's contemporary art at the Centro Párraga, and visit the Science and Water Museum for interactive exhibits.

Day 3: Day Trip to Cartagena.

- Morning: Travel to Cartagena (around 45 minutes by car or train). Explore the Roman Theatre and the National Museum of Underwater Archaeology.
- Lunch: Enjoy seafood by the harbor.
- Afternoon: Visit the Naval Museum and take a walk through the historic center.
- Evening: Return to Murcia.

Day 4: La Manga del Mar Menor.

- Morning: Drive to La Manga and enjoy the beautiful beaches and coastal activities.
- Lunch: Beachside restaurant.
- Afternoon: Continue exploring La Manga or try water sports.
- Evening: Return to Murcia for dinner.

Day 5: Sierra Espuña.

- Morning: Head to Sierra Espuña for hiking and nature trails.
- Lunch: Picnic in the mountains.
- Afternoon: Continue exploring the natural park.
- Evening: Return to Murcia.

Day 6: Ricote Valley.

- Morning: Explore the scenic Ricote Valley. Visit the charming villages of Archena and Ojós.
- Lunch: Local restaurant in the valley.
- Afternoon: Continue your tour of the valley, visiting vineyards and citrus groves.
- Evening: Return to Murcia for dinner.

Day 7: Relax and Reflect.

- Morning: Leisurely breakfast and visit any remaining sites of interest in Murcia.
- Lunch: Traditional Murcian restaurant.
- Afternoon: Enjoy a final walk around the city or some last-minute shopping.
- Evening: Dinner at a favorite spot and reflect on your trip.

Food and Wine Tour.

Day 1: Introduction to Murcian Cuisine.

- Morning: Start with a food market tour at Mercado de Verónicas. Sample fresh produce and local specialties.
- Lunch: Tapas crawl in the city center.
- Afternoon: Visit the Salzillo Museum.
- Evening: Dinner at a renowned restaurant, focusing on regional dishes.

Day 2: Wine and Vineyards.

- Morning: Take a guided tour to local vineyards in the Bullas wine region. Participate in wine tastings and learn about the winemaking process.
- Lunch: Vineyard restaurant or picnic.
- Afternoon: Continue exploring the vineyards.

- Evening: Return to Murcia and dine at a wine-focused restaurant.

Day 3: Cooking Classes and More.

- Morning: Join a cooking class to learn how to prepare traditional Murcian dishes.
- Lunch: Enjoy the meal you've prepared during the class.
- Afternoon: Visit a local olive oil farm or another culinary site.
- Evening: Dinner at a popular tapas bar.

Family Adventure.

Day 1: Fun and Learning.

- Morning: Terra Natura Murcia zoo and water park.
- Lunch: At the park.
- Afternoon: Science and Water Museum.
- Evening: Family-friendly restaurant.

Day 2: Nature and Play.

- Morning: Floridablanca Garden and playground.
- Lunch: Picnic or nearby café.
- Afternoon: Visit Murcia's Archaeological Museum for a kid-friendly tour.
- Evening: Dinner at a family-friendly restaurant.

Day 3: Day Trip to Lorca.

- Morning: Travel to Lorca and visit the Castle of Lorca, known as the Fortress of the Sun.
- Lunch: Local restaurant in Lorca.
- Afternoon: Explore the Archaeological Museum of Lorca.
- Evening: Return to Murcia for a relaxed family dinner.

Chapter 14: Travel Tips and FAQs

Navigating a new destination can be daunting, but with the right tips and answers to common questions, you can make the most of your trip to Murcia. This chapter covers essential travel tips, including common questions answered, do's and don'ts, money-saving strategies, sustainable travel practices, and advice for solo travelers.

Common Questions Answered.

What is the best time to visit Murcia?

The best times to visit Murcia are during the spring (March to May) and fall (September to November). The weather is pleasant, and there are various festivals and events. Summers can be very hot, while winters are mild but quieter in terms of tourism.

Do I need to speak Spanish to visit Murcia?

While knowing some basic Spanish phrases can be very helpful, many people in the tourism industry speak English. Learning a few key phrases can enhance your experience and is appreciated by locals.

Is Murcia safe for tourists?

Yes, Murcia is generally safe for tourists. As with any travel destination, exercise common sense, be aware of your surroundings, and take usual precautions to safeguard your belongings.

How do I get around Murcia?

Murcia has a well-connected public transportation system, including buses and trams. Taxis and ride-sharing services are also available. Walking and biking are great ways to explore the city center.

What should I pack for a trip to Murcia?

Pack according to the season. Light clothing for summer, layers for spring and fall, and a jacket for winter. Comfortable walking shoes, a hat, sunscreen, and a reusable water bottle are also recommended.

Do's and Don'ts.

Do's

- Respect Local Customs: Familiarize yourself with Spanish customs and etiquette. For example, greeting people with "Hola" and "Gracias" goes a long way.
- Try Local Cuisine: Sample traditional Murcian dishes and tapas. Visit local markets and food festivals.

- Stay Hydrated: Murcia can be hot, especially in summer, so drink plenty of water.
- Plan Ahead: Research the places you want to visit and check their opening hours and entry fees.

Don'ts.

- Avoid High Heat: During peak summer months, avoid outdoor activities during the hottest part of the day (12 pm to 4 pm).
- Don't Skip Siesta Time: Many shops and restaurants close in the early afternoon for siesta. Plan your activities around this.
- Respect Religious Sites: When visiting churches and cathedrals, dress modestly and respect the silence and rules of the place.
- Don't Expect Everything to Be Open on Sundays: Many stores and businesses may be closed or have reduced hours on Sundays.

Money-Saving Tips

- Use Public Transportation: Buses and trams are cheaper than taxis. Consider purchasing a travel card for discounts.
- Eat Like a Local: Dining at local bars and markets can be more affordable than touristy restaurants. Look for "menú del día" (menu of the day) for budget-friendly meals.

- Visit Free Attractions: Many museums and attractions have free entry on certain days or times. Check their websites for details.
- Shop at Local Markets: Buy fresh produce, snacks, and souvenirs from local markets instead of pricier shops.
- Stay in Budget Accommodations: Hostels, guesthouses, and budget hotels offer affordable lodging options.

Sustainable Travel Practices

- Reduce Plastic Use: Carry a reusable water bottle and shopping bag to minimize plastic waste.
- Support Local Businesses: Eat at locally-owned restaurants, buy from local artisans, and stay in eco-friendly accommodations.
- Conserve Resources: Be mindful of water and energy use in your accommodations. Turn off lights and air conditioning when not needed.
- Use Public Transportation or Walk: Reduce your carbon footprint by using public transit, biking, or walking instead of renting a car.
- Respect Nature: Stick to marked trails in natural parks, avoid disturbing wildlife, and dispose of waste properly.

Solo Travel Tips.

- Stay Connected: Keep friends or family informed of your whereabouts and share your itinerary with them.

- Join Group Tours: Group tours and activities are a great way to meet people and explore safely.

- Stay in Central Locations: Choose accommodations in central, well-lit areas that are close to public transport and main attractions.

- Trust Your Instincts: If a situation feels uncomfortable or unsafe, remove yourself and seek help if needed.

- Learn Basic Spanish Phrases: This can be helpful in emergencies and for everyday interactions.

By following these travel tips and advice, you can have a smooth, enjoyable, and memorable experience in Murcia.

Murcia Maps and Navigation.

Murcia City Center Map.

https://maps.app.goo.gl/ZqNoysE6UZuAWvis5

Murcia, Spain City Map

Scan QR code

Scanning a QR code is a straightforward process that typically involves using a smartphone or tablet. Here are five steps to scan a QR code:

Open the Camera App:
- Most modern smartphones have built-in QR code scanning functionality within the default camera app. Open the camera app on your smartphone.

Point the Camera at the QR Code:
- Position your device so that the QR code appears clearly within the frame. Make sure the entire code is visible and in focus.

Wait for the Camera to Recognize the Code:
- Hold your device steady and wait for a few seconds. The camera app should automatically recognize the QR code and display a notification or link on the screen.

Tap the Notification or Link:
- Once the QR code is recognized, a notification or link will pop up on your screen. Tap on it to open the associated content, which is the map.

Public Transport Maps.

https://maps.app.goo.gl/KQUNDsGWoq7WVUX96

Murcia, Public Transportation Map

Scan QR code

Scanning a QR code is a straightforward process that typically involves using a smartphone or tablet. Here are five steps to scan a QR code:

Open the Camera App:
- Most modern smartphones have built-in QR code scanning functionality within the default camera app. Open the camera app on your smartphone.

Point the Camera at the QR Code:
- Position your device so that the QR code appears clearly within the frame. Make sure the entire code is visible and in focus.

Wait for the Camera to Recognize the Code:
- Hold your device steady and wait for a few seconds. The camera app should automatically recognize the QR code and display a notification or link on the screen.

Tap the Notification or Link:
- Once the QR code is recognized, a notification or link will pop up on your screen. Tap on it to open the associated content, which is the map.

Walking Routes and Trails.

https://maps.app.goo.gl/3qjcP5JMfBPJsX6n7

Scan QR code

Scanning a QR code is a straightforward process that typically involves using a smartphone or tablet. Here are five steps to scan a QR code:

Open the Camera App:
- Most modern smartphones have built-in QR code scanning functionality within the default camera app. Open the camera app on your smartphone.

Point the Camera at the QR Code:
- Position your device so that the QR code appears clearly within the frame. Make sure the entire code is visible and in focus.

Wait for the Camera to Recognize the Code:
- Hold your device steady and wait for a few seconds. The camera app should automatically recognize the QR code and display a notification or link on the screen.

Tap the Notification or Link:
- Once the QR code is recognized, a notification or link will pop up on your screen. Tap on it to open the associated content, which is the map.

Emergency Services Map.

https://maps.app.goo.gl/AJaxkC8eVxQP1645A

Scan QR code

Scanning a QR code is a straightforward process that typically involves using a smartphone or tablet. Here are five steps to scan a QR code:

Open the Camera App:
- Most modern smartphones have built-in QR code scanning functionality within the default camera app. Open the camera app on your smartphone.

Point the Camera at the QR Code:
- Position your device so that the QR code appears clearly within the frame. Make sure the entire code is visible and in focus.

Wait for the Camera to Recognize the Code:
- Hold your device steady and wait for a few seconds. The camera app should automatically recognize the QR code and display a notification or link on the screen.

Tap the Notification or Link:
- Once the QR code is recognized, a notification or link will pop up on your screen. Tap on it to open the associated content, which is the map.

Murcia Top Attractions.

https://maps.app.goo.gl/B6tTqo5TUW13cB1y8

Scan QR code

Scanning a QR code is a straightforward process that typically involves using a smartphone or tablet. Here are five steps to scan a QR code:

Open the Camera App:
- Most modern smartphones have built-in QR code scanning functionality within the default camera app. Open the camera app on your smartphone.

Point the Camera at the QR Code:
- Position your device so that the QR code appears clearly within the frame. Make sure the entire code is visible and in focus.

Wait for the Camera to Recognize the Code:
- Hold your device steady and wait for a few seconds. The camera app should automatically recognize the QR code and display a notification or link on the screen.

Tap the Notification or Link:
- Once the QR code is recognized, a notification or link will pop up on your screen. Tap on it to open the associated content, which is the map.

Murcia Accommodations.

https://maps.app.goo.gl/R9X2qDtwALe9rLo58

Scan QR code

Scanning a QR code is a straightforward process that typically involves using a smartphone or tablet. Here are five steps to scan a QR code:

Open the Camera App:
- Most modern smartphones have built-in QR code scanning functionality within the default camera app. Open the camera app on your smartphone.

Point the Camera at the QR Code:
- Position your device so that the QR code appears clearly within the frame. Make sure the entire code is visible and in focus.

Wait for the Camera to Recognize the Code:
- Hold your device steady and wait for a few seconds. The camera app should automatically recognize the QR code and display a notification or link on the screen.

Tap the Notification or Link:
- Once the QR code is recognized, a notification or link will pop up on your screen. Tap on it to open the associated content, which is the map.

Conclusion

Thank you for embarking on this journey through the enchanting region of Murcia with us. "Murcia Travel Guide: Discover the Charm of Spain's Southeast" has been designed to be your comprehensive companion, offering insights, tips, and detailed information to help you explore and appreciate this unique part of Spain.

From the majestic Murcia Cathedral to the serene landscapes of Sierra Espuña, from the vibrant festivals that light up the city to the tranquil beaches of La Manga del Mar Menor, Murcia is a destination that captivates and delights at every turn. Its rich history, cultural heritage, and warm hospitality create an inviting atmosphere that makes every visitor feel at home.

We have delved into practical aspects such as transportation, accommodation, dining, and shopping to ensure your trip is seamless and enjoyable. Our curated itineraries aim to cater to a variety of interests, whether you're here for a day, a week, or looking for a family adventure or a culinary tour.

Murcia's charm lies not just in its landmarks but in the everyday experiences—the friendly conversations with locals, the discovery of hidden gems in bustling markets, the taste of perfectly cooked tapas, and the joy of a spontaneous dance at a local festival. It's these moments that turn a trip into a memorable journey.

As you set out to explore Murcia, remember to embrace the local customs, savor the regional flavors, and immerse yourself in the cultural rhythms that make this region so special. Whether you're wandering through historical sites, hiking in natural parks, or simply enjoying the sunshine by the coast, Murcia offers a rich tapestry of experiences that are waiting to be discovered.

We hope this guide has equipped you with the knowledge and inspiration to make the most of your visit. Travel with an open heart, respect the places you explore, and create your own unforgettable stories in this beautiful corner of Spain.

Safe travels, and may your adventures in Murcia be filled with joy, discovery, and lasting memories.

Made in the USA
Monee, IL
12 November 2024

69973079R00074